306.7

W9-CSD-672

DATE DUE

WITHDRAWN

GAYLORD			PRINTED IN U.S.A.

CARSON CITY LIBRARY

A GIFT FOR

_____

FROM

_____

Dr. Henry Cloud
& Dr. John Townsend

What to Do When You Don't Know What to Do

Sex & Intimacy

God Will Make a Way

INTEGRITY
PUBLISHERS

WHAT TO DO WHEN YOU DON'T KNOW WHAT TO DO:
SEX & INTIMACY

Copyright © 2005 by Henry Cloud and John Townsend.

Published by Integrity Publishers, a division of Integrity Media, Inc.,
5250 Virginia Way, Suite 110, Brentwood, TN 37027.

HELPING PEOPLE WORLDWIDE EXPERIENCE *the* MANIFEST PRESENCE
of GOD.

All rights reserved. No portion of this book may be reproduced, stored
in a retrieval system, or transmitted in any form or by any means—
electronic, mechanical, photocopy, recording, or any other—except for
brief quotations in printed reviews, without the prior written permission of the publisher.

Published in association with Yates & Yates, LLP, Literary Agents,
Orange, California.

Unless otherwise indicated, Scripture quotations are taken from The
Holy Bible, New International Version (NIV), copyright ©1973, 1978,
1984, International Bible Society. Used by permission of Zondervan
Bible Publishers.

Other Scripture quotations are taken from the following sources:

The New King James Version (NKJV), copyright ©1979, 1980, 1982,
Thomas Nelson, Inc., Publishers. Used by permission.

The Holy Bible, New Living Translation (NLT), copyright ©1996.
Used by permission of Tyndale House Publishers, Inc., Wheaton,
Illinois. All rights reserved.

Cover and interior design: UDG | DesignWorks,
www.udgdesignworks.com

ISBN 1-59145-352-6

Printed in the United States of America

05 06 07 08 09   LBM   9 8 7 6 5 4 3 2 1

Contents

Prologue

Sexual difficulties in marriage can be a devastating experience. Couples who find that their romantic intimacy isn't working—for whatever reason—go through tremendous emotional and relational pain. They wonder if they are really in love, or if they are damaged beyond repair. They start to give up hope that they will ever feel the completion and deep connection that comes with a loving and sexual marriage.

One couple I worked with, Dan and Linda, were almost at the end of their marriage because of a sexual conflict. Though she loved Dan, Linda simply had very little sexual desire for her husband.

She never approached him for sexual relations, and whenever he took the initiative, she would either try to avoid it or simply endure the experience. On his part, Dan was extremely hurt and frustrated by this and often felt like giving up on the relationship.

As I got to know the couple, I became aware of a pattern in their relationship that seemed significant. Though he loved Linda, Dan was pretty controlling with her. He told her what to do and "called the shots" quite often. And Linda seemed to simply take it. She took a more compliant and docile role, as it helped them to avoid butting heads and having conflict.

I knew that this sort of dance between two people often makes one spouse feel like a child and the other a parent. The "child" feels helpless and choiceless, and the "parent" feels in control and sometimes alone without an adult partner. Neither spouse feels really happy with the child-parent pattern.

I also knew that many problems in sexual unresponsiveness are associated with this pattern. Kids aren't designed to want to have sex with their parents, so often the powerless spouse can't feel arousal or desire. She can't access her adult libido with her mate.

I told Dan and Linda what I was thinking. Linda thought it made sense. Dan was a little resistant, until I said, "So you can decide to keep things as they are, feel in control, and not regain sex and passion. Or you can give up some of the power, give half to Linda, and stand a good chance of regaining the sexuality." When he saw it in that light, his incentive went up!

Dan began to encourage his wife's input, thoughts, and feelings. He stopped resisting her freedom as a person. Linda herself began to speak up more. She started disagreeing with Dan and confronting him when she needed to. It was a little rocky at first, for they weren't used to this. But pretty soon, Linda began feeling desire for Dan as she regained the adult role and position. Dan was grateful for the changes and felt that he'd had to give up very little to have a great marriage restored. I agreed with his analysis. It is also a symbol of a deep spiritual reality: what we give up to God, we are repaid for many times over.

There are many other sexual problems besides Linda's lack of responsiveness, such as impotence and premature ejaculation. We will go into some of the specifics a bit later. These can be bewildering and discouraging. But they are real.

However, if you are having sexual conflicts in your relationship, take heart. God makes a way for us all, in every path of life, and that includes the sexual arena. He created and designed the sexual experience, and he is very much "for" it. He has provided answers for your struggle in this book, and they work—if you engage in the process. Listen to him, learn from him . . . and watch what happens to the sex you have wanted to experience.

PART I:
EIGHT PRINCIPLES TO GUIDE YOU TOWARD GREATER INTIMACY AND BETTER SEX IN YOUR MARRIAGE

Many married couples are surprised when they face sexual problems. Sex is so natural, so much a part of love, that they cannot understand how it became so difficult and complex. Before marriage they anticipated sex as a delightful playground. But now it has become a battleground. And their disappointment is all the worse because in sex they had such high expectations of ecstasy. If this describes you in any way, be sure that God has a way for you to restore the joy of your sexual relationship.

You can find God's way back to sexual pleasure when you activate your faith in him by following the eight principles in this section. We will have more to say specifically about working on particular sexual problems in the section that follows this one. Think of these principles as foundation stones. You must lay them in your life so that you can build on them the structures you need to win over your problem.

Begin Your Journey with God

W hen we speak of God, we don't mean some kind of vague, universal force; we mean a real person, complete with mind, will, and the power to act in our lives. So when we say that faith and trust will carry you to a resolution of your sexual problem, we're not talking about warm religious feelings or an exercise in positive thinking. Meaningful faith must be placed in a real Person, who knows the way for you and promises to lead you on it. That's God. So our first principle for healing is to *begin your journey with God.* You can't do it without him.

Your need for God's help is no more a weakness than your need for air. We did not create ourselves, nor were we designed to create our own way in life. God wired us to depend on him. When you exercise faith in him, you position yourself to accomplish superhuman feats. You are reaching beyond human strength and knowledge and tapping into God's infinite strength and knowledge. After all, the designer of sexuality knows how to fix it when it goes wrong.

Most of us, when facing a difficult or painful situation that we don't know how to handle, do one of two things. First, we repeat what didn't work before, but this time we try harder. Chronic dieters, for example, try to muster up just a little more will power, and "this time it will work." Second, we stop trying altogether. *I will never stop overeating, so what's the use?* The first reaction often spawns the second. Trying to get through life on your own limited strength and knowledge leads to futility and loss of hope.

But in God's economy, getting to the end of yourself is the beginning of hope. Jesus said, "God blesses those who realize their need for him" (Matthew 5:3 NLT). When you admit your helplessness and ask God for help, you transcend your own limitations and God's resources become available to you.

God's resources cannot be earned; they can only be received as a gift when we, in humility, acknowledge our need for our Creator. He is ready to get involved in your life. All you have to do is say yes to him. Then he will provide what you need to overcome the effects of even the most miserable sexual problem.

Sometimes his way will be truly miraculous, and sometimes it will involve a lot of work and change on your part. Often it won't be the way you thought you needed. But when God makes a way, it works.

People who

rise to the top seldom

get there alone.

They seek help.

2

Choose Your Traveling Companions Wisely

When I (Henry) was a youngster, Jack Nicklaus was king of golf, and as an aspiring golfer, I thought he was almost a god. Then I heard that he consulted a golf pro for help on his swing. I was stunned. Teachers were for people who didn't know what they were doing. I have learned a lot since then. People who rise to the top seldom get there alone. They seek help.

This story illustrates our second principle of God's way of solving problems: *Surround yourself*

One of the ways God works is through other people.

with people who are committed to support you, encourage you, assist you, and pray for you. Of course, when sexuality is the issue, remain sensitive to the private nature of the problem and open up to those who can be trusted not to embarrass your mate. When the problem is severe enough, and certainly when it's a relationship problem in some other area of your marriage that affects your sex life, you and your mate can find strength in support and help from others.

One of the ways God works is through other people. Solomon said, "Two are better than one. . . . If one falls down, his friend can help him up. But pity the man who falls and has no one to help him up!" (Ecclesiastes 4:9–10). Some of these people will just show up in your life, sent at just the right time. Others you have to seek out. They can range from professionals to a neighbor or friend at church. Here are some important qualities to look for as you select your support team.

SUPPORT. The loss of sexual ability may leave you feeling hopeless. It can drain you of emotional, physical, and spiritual strength. You need the kind of person who will understand and find ways to help you.

LOVE. You need the safety net of people who love you deeply just as you are, even when you don't feel lovable.

COURAGE. You will encounter risk and fear. When the task looks too daunting to face, your support team will build your courage.

FEEDBACK. You can't see yourself objectively. You need honest people who are not afraid to correct you when you are wrong.

WISDOM. You don't have all the wisdom and knowledge you need to make it. Look for wise people through whom God will speak to you.

EXPERIENCE. Seek out the experience of others who have been through the problem and know what you are going through.

MODELING. It is difficult to do what we have never seen done. Learn from those who have successfully conquered the problem you are facing.

VALUES. Your value system will guide you as you work through the problem. We learn values from others, and others support us by enforcing values. Stay close to people who share your values; stay away from those who don't.

ACCOUNTABILITY. You need people who will monitor your progress and keep you on track. Look for people who will ask the tough questions: Where are you failing? What kind of help do you need?

You may already have in your life people who meet your need for support. If so, explain that you need them on your present journey. Ask if they will be available to provide accountability, feedback, or support. They will probably feel honored and valued that you would ask.

If you run short of supportive friends, consider joining a structured support system, such as a Bible study group. Share with these people your relationship struggle (though not the intimate details of your sex life or your partner's sexual failures) and ask for their prayers and input. You will be amazed how a loving support group will help you on your journey.

A key way out of despair is to

find missing pieces of

wisdom and apply them

to your problem.

3

Place High Value on Wisdom

Often we feel hopeless and don't know how to resolve our sexual problems because we lack vital information about them. A key way out of despair is to find these missing pieces of wisdom and apply them to our problem. God tells us that wisdom produces hope: "Know also that wisdom is sweet to your soul; if you find it, there is a future hope for you, and your hope will not be cut off" (Proverbs 24:14).

So our third principle for finding God's way to overcome sexual problems is this: *Recognize the value and need for the missing pieces of wisdom in your life; then ask God to show them to you.*

WISDOM COMES FROM GOD. James tells us to ask God for the wisdom we need: "If any of you lacks wisdom, he should ask God, who gives generously to all without finding fault . . ." (James 1:5). God knows what to do even when you don't. Ask him for answers and he will provide them.

GOD USES OTHERS. You may not know how to handle your situation, but there is somebody out there who does. Find that someone. Whenever I (Henry) am dealing with a difficult financial situation, I call a certain friend who has great wisdom in that area, and I lean on him for good advice. I have other people I call for other needs.

When facing a sexual difficulty, you are wise to seek out people who have knowledge, expertise, and experience in that area—people who know how to lead you through it.

SEEK STRUCTURED WISDOM. Often, overcoming sexual problems requires more than good advice from friends or others. You may need structured and professional sources of wisdom. And there are a great number of services out there, including trained counselors, support groups, physicians, and psychiatrists. You don't need to reinvent the wheel for your situation. There is help available, already in place.

Here is a sampling of places to start looking:

- Professionals in your area of need

- Self-help groups

- Pastors

- Community colleges

- Seminars

- Books, tapes, and videos

- Healthy conferences on marriage that include sexual issues

One caution: Make sure the resources you uncover are authentic. Get referrals from people you trust—your friends, your support group, your doctor, or your pastor.

THE ORDER OF THINGS. God has put you in a universe of order. Things work because of the laws God set in place at creation, and this includes sexuality. Part of the way for you to restore your sex life has already been made in how he created life to work. Your task is to find the wisdom that is already there. So search for his wisdom with all your strength and apply it wholeheartedly.

4

Leave Your Baggage Behind

We all hate dragging a million pieces of luggage through a crowded airport. What if you had to tote a couple of suitcases, backpacks, and carry-on bags everywhere you went? It would weigh you down and hold you back.

It's the same in the sex life of your marriage. Emotional baggage can weigh you down and hold you back. Our fourth principle for finding God's way to overcome sexual problems is to *leave your baggage behind.*

By baggage we mean bad stuff from the past. We've all experienced difficult events and relationships, emotional hurts, serious mistakes, tragic accidents, or loss of a loved one. Ideally, these events are resolved as they happen. But often pain is stuffed instead of dealt with; offenders are not forgiven; fears are not confronted; conflicts are not resolved, leaving us with past feelings and patterns of behavior that impact the present. That's baggage. You can be sure that baggage will cause certain sexual problems, and you can't be fully healed until you deal with it. In fact, the reality is that most sexual issues are not medical or physical in nature, though some are. Most have to do with emotional or relational issues, which certainly makes baggage relevant.

Here are five practical tips for helping you discard baggage.

1. AGREE THAT YOU HAVE A PAINFUL PAST. Acknowledge that a painful thing has happened to you, involving issues that were not resolved. If

you don't work through them, they will prevent your healing. So the first step is to confess to yourself and to God that you have these issues.

2. INCLUDE OTHERS IN YOUR HEALING AND GRIEVING. Seek from others the care and healing you need to resolve these issues. Pouring out your hurt to others who love you opens the door to comfort, encouragement, healing, and support.

3. RECEIVE FORGIVENESS. Getting rid of baggage means being free of the guilt and shame of past failures and sins. God will forgive you for anything you have ever done, no matter how bad. The Bible promises, "For as high as the heavens are above the earth, so great is his love for those who fear him; as far as the east is from the west, so far has he removed our transgressions from us" (Psalm 103:11–12).

Your past failures and mistakes may also have alienated you from certain people. You must go to them, humbly confess your wrong, and receive

> You still carry pain, anger, and perhaps hatred. You must forgive these people.

forgiveness. Once you know you are forgiven, accepted, and loved, you can then re-enter life and begin moving on.

4. FORGIVE OTHERS. Some of your baggage may be hurts you received from others, perhaps your former spouse. You still carry pain, anger, and perhaps hatred. You must forgive these people. Take your cue from God, who has forgiven you. If you don't forgive, resentment will eat away at your heart. When you forgive another, you release that person from your right to exact punishment and retribution from them. As well, you release your own baggage of pain and resentment in the process.

5. SEE YOURSELF THROUGH NEW EYES. Another kind of baggage is the distorted view of ourselves we learned in past relationships or situations. We tend to see ourselves through the eyes

of others who are important to us. And depending on whether that view is positive or negative, we either feel valued or devalued. A realistic self-view will be balanced, recognizing strengths as well as weaknesses and growth areas.

Find this view by seeing yourself through God's eyes, for he loves you unconditionally and values you highly. Add to this the view you get from those who love you as God does. Let this *new you* replace the distorted picture that has caused you such grief.

Holding on to the baggage of the past will disable your resolution of relationship problems that can impair your sex life. Ask God to help you leave it behind.

In your life,

the buck stops with you.

When addressing any problem,

you need to step up

to the plate and take charge.

5

Own Your Faults and Weaknesses

I n your life, the buck stops with you. When addressing the problems that arise in the sexual area, you need to step up to the plate and take charge. It's your job to do what God gives you to do. And it's your job to accept the blame for the failures that are truly your own failures, not someone else's. Our fifth principle for God's way to sexual recovery is that you *take responsibility for your life, own up to your faults, and accept blame where it is justified.*

The apostle Paul wrote, "Continue to work out your salvation with fear and trembling, for it is God

> Sometimes we have to take responsibility for situations that are not our fault.

who works in you to will and to act according to his good purpose" (Philippians 2:12–13). Now that God has saved you, it's your responsibility to live a life that reflects him. But notice that you are not alone in your efforts. God is there with you, empowering you. And this partnership between you and him accomplishes your goal.

Sometimes we have to take responsibility for situations that are not our fault. The man who is unfairly laid off must own up to the situation and start looking for another job. The abused wife must seek counseling.

Determining who is the primary cause of the problem isn't as important as determining who will do something about it. The latter "who" is you. Whichever of you has the problem, if it affects your sex life, it's a problem that belongs to both of you. What matters is taking ownership to correct the problem. If it's his problem, he should take steps to correct it. He needs her support and encouragement, and if he does not take the needed steps, she needs to take initiative to urge him to do it. And the same applies to the husband when the problem is with the wife. Remember that Dan had to own his control, and Linda had to own her compliance.

When we take ownership for what happens in our lives, we are empowered to make changes—to develop plans, tackle situations, and right wrongs. People who take charge of their lives are active people with real initiative. Ownership also frees us from false hopes, from discouragement and passivity, and to take risks and test-drive possible solutions.

When you take ownership and invite God to move in, he does it. He will get involved in moving you to success in restoring your sex life. Our role is to seek him, take charge of our own circumstances, and trust him to do for us what only he can do.

Welcome your problems

as gifts from God

to help you

become a better person.

Embrace Problems as Gifts

S ome people hit a problem and stop dead in their tracks—they feel stuck and hopeless. All they want is to get rid of it as soon as possible. Other people find something useful in problems. They ask, "What can I learn from this experience? What does God want to change in me?" This is our sixth principle for finding God's way through sexual problems: *Welcome your problems as gifts from God to help you become a better person.*

There's nothing wrong with trying to solve a problem and alleviate the pain. But instead of rushing to the most immediate fix, we must use the problem to see our lives from God's perspective and find God's way through it.

And God's perspective is quite different—as different as the way a physician and a patient view pain. You come to the doctor in agony wanting a shot or a pill to make the pain go away. And you want it *now.* But your physician knows your pain is a sign of a deeper problem. He prescribes even more pain: surgery and physical therapy.

It's a choice all of us have to make at some point: You can demand immediate relief, knowing that your problem will recur. Or you can go through the healing process and resolve the problem once and for all. That's the choice you face when dealing with the pain of sexual problems. God loves you, and like your physician, he is less concerned about your immediate comfort than about your long-term health.

The Bible tells us, "Consider it pure joy, my brothers, whenever you face trials of many kinds, because you know that the testing of your faith develops perseverance" (James 1:2–3). God's way is not *out* of your problem but *through* it. That's how we learn from our difficulties and find God's way.

As you experience the pain of sexual difficulties and don't know what to do about them, you first need to look upward, toward God. He is like a storm raining down on a stagnant stream clogged with debris. As the torrent floods the stream, the debris is broken up and the flow resumes.

Second, you must look *inward*. Let God take you on a journey into yourself. He will shine a lantern of truth into the recesses of your heart, illuminating attitudes, wounds, hurts, weaknesses, and perspectives where you need to submit to his touch.

Problems are also a gift in that they help us *normalize* pain—to expect it as a regular part of life. We tend to think that bad things shouldn't happen to us, and we react in anger, denial, or despair when they do. But this doesn't alter the reality of the pain.

You must give up your protest about the unfairness of your problem and come to a place of acceptance. Only then can you learn what choices, paths, lessons, and opportunities are available to you. Accept pain as part of life. Accept that you don't have all the answers. Acceptance helps us to adapt to the way things really are, and to trust God.

Our problems help us identify with Jesus's sufferings. He loves us deeply, and our rebellion hurts him. But instead of finding a way out, he works through it. While he redeems, restores, and forgives us, he suffers. But he endures it because it's the only way. That is our model for dealing with pain. Identifying with his pain draws us closer to him, to see life as it really is and patiently take whatever steps are necessary to resolve the problem. Following the pattern of Jesus deepens and matures us.

You should not just passively accept the pain caused by your sexual difficulty as the way things will always be, but neither should you ask God to just make the symptoms vanish instantly. Work through it God's way, and accept the gift of what you learn from the process.

We must allow time

for God to work.

Take Life as It Comes

I (John) have a bone disease called osteopenia. My bones are too porous, and they break easier than normal bones. I am on a special diet and a regimen of bone-strengthening exercises. I get an annual x-ray to check my progress. I would love to get more frequent progress reports, but bones change too slowly for that. The waiting is difficult, but it has taught me that I am not the master of time. I can't speed it up. I must let time have its way.

Our seventh principle for following God's way relates to what I am learning through my osteopenia: *we must allow time for God to work.* Though

Time heals
nothing
in and of itself.

I believe that God performs instantaneous miracles, it seems that his norm is a time-consuming process. Therefore, you must allow time for his process to happen.

Still, it's not easy to wait. When things don't happen quickly, we tend to become impatient, frustrated, and ready to give up. However, those who insist on shortcuts and quick fixes tend to repeat the same problems over and over, getting nowhere. In the arena of sexual problems, this is an important reality. Time, patience, vulnerability, change, and risk are all part of the process, and you must accept and deal with that reality. People are often afraid, ashamed, and embarrassed to take risks sexually. That is normal. Give the process time.

We need to add a thought here, however. You've heard the saying "Time heals all wounds."

Time heals nothing in and of itself. It's futile to wait passively for God to change circumstances, for help to appear, or for your feelings to change. Such inaction will stick you in a holding pattern where you'll become discouraged when healing doesn't occur. You don't simply wait for a sprained knee to heal. You get a brace and do the physical therapy. Time is the context for our involvement in the process. When you invite God into your life and participate with him in the process, you will begin to see results. So do your part. Seek help and get into the process required for healing. The more engaged you are, the less you will feel the pressure of time.

As nature has seasons, so do our lives. Solomon wrote, "There is a time for everything, and a season for every activity under heaven" (Ecclesiastes 3:1). We can better understand God's timing when we understand the seasons of our lives and identify which we are in.

WINTER. Cold weather and hard ground make things appear dead and unfruitful, but winter can be a very productive time. It's a time to clear out the deadwood, debris, and stones that will hinder future growth; to mend fences and repair broken machinery; to plan and prepare for the growing seasons.

Arrange your schedule and set goals. Research the resources you need, such as programs and counselors. Use winter to prepare. Pray for sexual healing to start.

SPRING. It's a time of new beginnings and fresh hope. You plow the soil, add fertilizer and supplements, plant seeds, and irrigate. You care for the fragile shoots that appear, keeping the garden free of destructive pests.

In the spring of your life, you implement the plans you made in the winter. Take some actions to talk to those with experience. Seek a counselor, find a group, read books, and get connected and informed.

SUMMER. In summer the fields are lush with healthy plants. It's a season for maintenance and protection of what you began in the spring. Don't be lulled into inactivity because good things are happening. Stay with the program; keep working at what God has given you to do. In sexual issues, this might mean that you are beginning to realize some changes and results. Don't stop. The process will most likely need to be fulfilled for sexual results to be permanent.

FALL. At harvesttime you reap what you have sown. You experience and enjoy the benefits of your work. Love, relationship, and sex all combine to create a beautiful connection of passion between you two. Have a party!

In the fall of personal growth, you see victory in the battle over your sexual problem. It's a time of celebration and gratitude. It's a time to give back to God and others something of what you have received.

We would all rather skip the work of winter, spring, and summer and enjoy the harvest of fall all the time. But the only way to reap a bountiful harvest is to make good use of your time in each season.

Love God with All You Are

God loves you unconditionally, and even if you have no clue about how to recover a joyful sex life, he has a way for you to do it. Following his way is a matter of love on your part. Our eighth principle for following God's way is to *love him passionately with every area of your life.*

Jesus said, "Love the Lord your God with all your heart and with all your soul and with all your mind. This is the first and greatest commandment" (Matthew 22:37–38). Loving God is the greatest commandment because it encompasses all the others. If we love God, connect to him, and do what honors him, we will find that we are also doing what is best for us. Immerse yourself in his love, and you will find his way to victory.

Here are a few facets of your life where love for God must take the lead.

VALUES. Our values determine what is important to us. Loving God means what is important to him should be important to you.

PASSIONS. These deep urges and drives make us feel alive. Let your love for God fuel your passions.

EMOTIONS. No matter how you feel in your situation—afraid, anxious, sad, or angry—ask God to reach inside you with his love so that you will be able to feel your feelings in ways that help you grow and move on.

TALENTS. Love God with all your strengths, skills, and abilities. As you do, God will use you to make a way for others.

Think of the dearest, closest, most loving relationship you have ever had in your life. What characterized this relationship? You were probably very open and vulnerable with each other. You knew each other's secrets, fears, and desires. You took risks with each other. You needed and depended on each other. And this relationship made you feel alive.

Our best human relationships are only a frail picture of the loving, intimate relationship you can enjoy with God. Learning to love him with everything you are is a lifelong journey. And the more of yourself you open up to him, the more God is able to help you through the bad times.

Loving God is saying to him, "Do whatever you need to do in my life." This gives him access to every part of you that needs his love, grace, and support.

You may feel connected to God in your head, theologically, but not your heart, emotionally. Or the converse may be true. Either way, begin to bring those aspects of your soul and life to his grace so that all of you is being loved and supported by God himself.

If you ever need God's way in your life, it's when you experience the pain and despair of impaired sex. God has the will and the resources to put your sex life back together. "He heals the brokenhearted and binds up their wounds" (Psalm 147:3). However, you must bring your problem to God in order to experience his love and healing.

God is all about love, and he wants us to be all about love too. The more you make everything you are accessible to him, the more you can grow, be healed, and find his way. Be sure you are not hiding the pain of your sexual difficulties from God. Love God with your heart, soul, mind, and strength, and let his love set you free.

PART II:
INTIMACY AND SEX

Sometimes when I (John) am speaking to a group about marriage, I will reverse a stereotype to see if everyone is awake. I'll say, "You women just don't get it. All you have on your mind is sex, and we guys just want to be held. Can you imagine what it's like for us to feel like such an object?" Most of the time, people will look at each other with amusement, as if to say, "Yeah, right."

Sex is a significant part of being involved in the life of God. We are sexual beings, and God authored and designed sexuality for our good. Sex can result in the creation of children, it brings closeness to a marriage, and it symbolizes God's love for us. God is clearly in the bedroom, and he wants to make that room a place where love, relationship, and his presence belong and are integrated together. If you are experiencing sexual problems that you don't know how to handle, he can make a way for you to develop a healthy sexual relationship in your marriage.

A GOD THING

Sexuality reflects the nature and heart of God. It is truly a God thing. Sex is deeply rooted in relationship, as God is. A satisfying, intimate sexual life is always built on a foundation of emotional connectedness and love between a wife and a husband. The better the relationship between the two, the stronger the likelihood of great sex. When a husband's eyes meet his wife's during the intimacy of those moments, they are looking into each other's souls. They are reaping the harvest of all the years they have spent in getting to know each other and celebrating the love that has blossomed, grown, and deepened between them. They are promising and anticipating a future of even more love, surprises, and new horizons in their union. Sex both reflects and develops love. The two belong not to themselves, but to each other: "My lover is mine and I am his" (Song of Songs 2:16).

Sex, like God, has a mystery to it that we cannot fully understand. Though we know a great deal about the mechanics of sex, we cannot fathom every aspect of the depth of the attraction between the sexes. So much is involved—from the subtle eye contact that can convey worlds of meaning, to the gradual progression of increasing involvement, to the sexual act itself, with all its tenderness, passion, and energy. Its shape and form at any particular time cannot be predicted: romantic and sweet, aggressive and powerful, recreational and athletic, quietly or outrageously humorous, or so deep and vulnerable that it can bring a couple to tears.

That two can become one is a mystery. The sexual union symbolizes the fact that two people,

> Sex brings together the "sacred" and the "secular."

though still distinct individuals and souls, have merged their lives to create a new and unique entity in marriage. Scripture states it this way: "For this reason a man will leave his father and mother and be united to his wife, and they will become one flesh" (Genesis 2:24). The sexual act itself portrays this oneness. The sexual climax, one of the greatest and most intense physical sensations we can experience, involves a temporary loss of separate identities and an emotional merger into the other person. Sexual union also symbolizes, at the highest level, Christ's union with his bride, the church (Ephesians 5:32).

Sex also has a timeless quality. Research tells us that people can be sexually active much later in life than we once thought. While some couples who have been married a short time have a sad, dying sex life, others who have been together for many years still enjoy sexual intimacy as an important and regular part of the marriage. Long past the childbearing years, they connect at the sexual level for closeness, recreation, and a celebration of God's care for them. The difference between these couples has more to do with the character and qualities of the people and the relationship than with their age.

Sex brings together the "sacred" and the "secular." As counselors we always feel very sad when we hear of couples or individuals who have felt forced to bring their sexual concerns to someone outside of the church because their own Christian community's attitude about sex was that it was something dirty. The view of the Church Lady on *Saturday Night Live,* with her crusade against sexuality, does not represent what the Bible teaches about the topic. God, the Author of sex, talks about it in extremely positive and graphic terms: "May your fountain be blessed, and may you rejoice in the wife of your youth. A loving doe, a graceful deer—may her breasts satisfy you always, may you ever be captivated by her love" (Proverbs 5:18–19).

Throughout the ages other religions have included sex with their worship. Though they did not understand what God's full design was, they seemed to sense that there is a quality to sex that brings us out of our routine existence. Sex makes us feel and experience something larger than ourselves, and at its best—in a deeply rooted and connected marriage—it gives us, for a few moments, a sliver of a glimpse into the face of God.

BODY AND SOUL

Sex cannot be cleanly parsed into either physical or emotional terms. It is sensual. It is anatomical. It is spiritual. It brings all parts of life together and is described by experts as being *psychophysiological*— that is, both psychological and physiological in nature. Sex involves our brain and neurological functions as much as it does our emotions and passions. Sexuality gives us a wonderful image of how God integrates body and soul, physical and emotional. Both the physical and nonphysical aspects of our being long to be connected to God (Psalm 63:1); he is involved with all of our being. We have truly been "fearfully and wonderfully made" (Psalm 139:14).

Sex researchers and clinicians have brought home this spiritual reality in the past few decades. They have found that sexual problems are rarely isolated to only one part of a person's life; they often have a physiological, emotional, or relational component. For instance, impotency can be caused by diabetes or atherosclerosis, and premature ejaculation is sometimes helped by antidepressants. It's also true that if a wife feels that her husband is attracted to her only sexually, she may lose interest in sex because she feels like an object. Couples can be quite physically healthy and active, but if they have severe discord in the relationship, their sex life may be nonexistent.

In other words, it is often what is underlying the sexual relationship—the heart of the person or the fabric of the marriage—that is the real issue. You can have a clean bill of health from your physician and know all the sexual techniques you should know, and still have sexual problems. Sex can't be disconnected from our souls. If there are hurts or problems in the soul, they will often manifest themselves in the sexual area of marriage.

In addition, God made us sexual beings, apart from the act itself. Being sexual has much more to it than the act of sex. The arena of sexuality is one of the many ways we experience ourselves and others. Just as we notice other people's personalities, styles, career paths, and family situations, we also notice them sexually: how attractive or unattractive they are, whether they are covert or overt, as well as other areas of sexuality. We need to keep the sexual part of ourselves connected to God, our values, and our support community in order to receive guidance in dealing with the realities of sexual temptation and desire, for when "desire has conceived, it gives birth to sin" (James 1:15). However, whether our sexuality is integrated into our soul or is out of control, it is still a part of us.

This spiritual connection of body and soul forms the context of the sexual act. Orgasm—technically the end result of the act of sex—is best viewed as a part of the whole, including tenderness, communication, nonsexual body pleasuring, and closeness. Because of this, some sexual experiences will not necessarily end in orgasm but simply in arousal and intimacy. (Husbands, pay attention here!) In and of itself, an orgasm is somewhat of a nonevent. Orgasm without relationship, closeness, communication, and love is not truly a meaningful experience between a husband and a wife. Sex is not about orgasm; it is about two becoming one. It's God's desire that you experience all the joy that surrounds this mystery.

WHAT CAN GO WRONG?

If either you or your partner are experiencing sexual problems, that means your marriage is experiencing sexual problems. Sex, as one of God's greatest gifts, is important to our well-being, and it should never be dismissed as mere expendable pleasure and unimportant to the relationship. Sexual problems are not to be ignored and accepted; they are to be faced and dealt with. If you don't know how to get back the joy in the area of sex, God can make a way for you to do it. And he wants to do it.

The first step is to understand the problem. You must know what you are facing before you can overcome it. Therefore, before we continue, we will present the categories of sexual problems and dysfunctions that couples can experience.

First, there are problems with *desire*, meaning that a person has little appetite for a sexual relationship. For example, a woman may believe that sex is a good thing and even perform sexually, but not experience an internal desire for it. This problem can occur at different degrees of severity and for varying lengths of time. Some people have never felt any desire for sex. Others will experience diminished libido after a loss, a life problem, or a medical issue. Still others, while having sexual appetites in general, will for some reason have no desire for their spouse.

The second category of sexual difficulties concerns *arousal.* God made our bodies to prepare themselves for sex in physiological ways. A woman's vagina begins to lubricate, and her genitals begin swelling. A man's penis becomes erect. When there are arousal dysfunctions, these elements of sexual functioning do not occur as they should. The woman's lack of lubrication can make intercourse very painful for her. The man's lack of an adequate erection, also called impotence, makes penetration impossible.

The third category of sexual problems has to do with *orgasm.* A woman may be either unable to experience an orgasm or find that it takes a very long time to climax. A man may have the same problem, or the reverse, which is *premature ejaculation*, a condition in which he climaxes too quickly.

These terms are not precise. There is a wide range of what is normal, healthy, and satisfying to an individual and to a couple in terms of how frequently they desire sex and can be aroused, and how long it takes to reach orgasm. A lot has to do with finding what makes the couple happy or unhappy, and why.

Sexual addictions are an increasingly visible sign of a marriage in trouble. (Technically, sexual addiction is not a true addiction, but more of a dependency.) In these situations, the spouse (more often it is the husband) is spending time on pornography, on telephone hot lines with sexual content, at strip clubs, or in prostitution. This is a heartbreaking situation, as the wife must bear the pain of being betrayed, as well as being deceived by the one with whom she has covenanted her life. This is not a small problem.

The man may attempt to justify his indiscretions by blaming his wife's lack of sexual attractiveness or responsiveness. In reality, the difficulty is not with her, nor is it really with sex either. It generally has to do with some part of him that is disconnected from relationship and life. Sometimes it is a sexualized wish for comfort and validation. In other cases, it is a desire for power, control, or choices. In still other cases, the man may have a conflict between his real self and his ideal self that he cannot reconcile. Or he may be angry and rebellious against what he perceives as the controlling nature of the women in his life.

In these instances, not only does the wife need to realize that it is her husband's issue, not hers, but she also needs to seek outside help and insist that he get help. Such assistance is available, and it works, but the husband must become involved. The wife needs to use every resource and person available to influence him to get help.

In addition, there are other sexual problems that a spouse—husband or wife—might have that can greatly disturb the marital connection, such as gender identity issues. While we will not deal with these problems in this little book, people facing them can find a great deal of hope and help, both personally and as a couple, with trained professionals who have expertise in these areas.

Now that we've dealt with the spiritual core of sexuality and summarized some of the sexual problems that can occur in marriage, let's turn our focus to what it takes to have a healthy sex life, and how couples who are struggling sexually can rekindle sexual passion.

LOVE: THE FOUNDATION

A healthy sex life begins with love. Love brings a couple together and allows sex to flourish. Love encompasses sex; it's larger than sex.

Love can create the desire for sex, but when the momentary passion of sex is over, love remains. It continues and is present with the couple, holding them close to each other and to the Author of love himself.

A large part of sexual love is *knowing*. The Bible refers to Adam and Eve's sexual relationship with a Hebrew word that means "to know" (Genesis 4:1, NKJV), and it indicates a personal understanding and knowledge of the other person. Sexual love is about knowing your spouse, personally and intimately. That means you should know your partner's feelings, fears, secrets, hurts, and dreams, and care about them. And likewise, your partner should know and care about yours.

The vulnerability of sex increases that base of knowing, as husband and wife reveal their innermost souls to each other through sexual love. By its unveiling and exposed nature, sex demands that sort of openness. In sexual intimacy two

Love involves the
whole person:
heart, soul,
mind, and strength.

people show each other the privacy of their bodies as well as the privacy of their hearts and feelings.

Love involves the whole person: heart, soul, mind, and strength (Mark 12:30). Love and sex both require an emotional connection between two people, which means both should be emotionally present and available. When two people can attach to each other in their hearts, a healthy sex life will emerge and develop. Yet when a couple lacks this kind of intimacy, their sex life will become atrophied because it cannot feed off the emotional connection. This can happen in several ways. Sometimes one mate will withdraw love out of anger, hurt, or a desire to punish the other. At other times one will be unable to take in or receive the other's love. Still other times one mate may have an inability to live emotionally in the world. Both people's hearts must be available in order to connect emotionally. If this is not the case, while sex can occur, it more often than not does not have enough fuel to be enflamed.

It's also true that love, and healthy sexuality, cannot exist without trust. Because sex is such a symbol of personal exposure and vulnerability, a healthy sex life requires that couples develop a great deal of trust in each other—trust that one partner will not use what he or she knows to hurt the other. When people trust each other, they feel free to continue their explorations of one another at deeper and deeper levels. In fact, one of the Hebrew words for trust also means "careless." In other words, when you trust someone, you can, in one sense, be *careless* with him or her. Of course, by careless we don't mean you can neglect the other's needs and feelings, but rather that you need not be anxious and fearful, editing what you say and feel. You are free to be yourself with the other person, because you can trust that he or she will not do wrong by you.

On the other hand, broken trust will often create sexual problems. This breach of trust doesn't even have to involve anything in the sexual arena, such as an affair or emotional unfaithfulness, though these can certainly be devastating to a relationship. A breach of trust can have to do with a financial matter, such as not being dependable with money, or it may be a commitment matter, such as promising something and not following through with it.

Broken trust can greatly diminish a person's desire for sex with a spouse. The deficit in emotional safety translates into a deficit in sexual safety. Broken trust can also affect a woman's ability to achieve orgasm, for a woman's sexual climax requires a great deal of willingness to lose control. If a wife is afraid she can't be "careless" with her husband in some area, she may be unable to let go of her own controls because of her fear. All of the techniques in the world will not cure a sexual problem caused by a breach of trust. Only God's solution of repentance, ownership, and rebuild-ing trustworthiness can accomplish it.

Love also changes our focus. It shifts our per-spective from an emphasis on "I" to a focus on "we." That is, in love, the whole is truly greater than the sum of its parts. It is not self-seeking (1 Corinthians 13:5); it is relationship-seeking. That's why couples don't talk about building their *lives* together. They discuss and dream about building a *life* together. There is a continual emphasis on how "we" are and on caring for the other person's welfare. Love is the ultimate cure for self-centeredness and narcissism.

This identification as "we" means a great deal sexually. It means that your spouse desires you, pursues you, and wants to be closer to you. In other words, when you identify yourself as "we" rather than "I," you will see that the more you have of your spouse, the better off you are. It means that you want to know your partner better, more deeply, to become closer in every way, and to invest your life in knowing who the two of you are as a couple. This is fertile soil from which a great sex life sprouts.

I have a friend who has discovered that when he talks with his wife about "our life together" and "what we want," it is a great aphrodisiac. He's not being manipulative—he means what he is saying to her—and his wife is aware that he uses phrases like this instead of "you" and "me" when discussing their goals, desires, and team efforts. Of course, when they discuss themselves as separate people, he doesn't blur their identities either. At any rate, his wife is a very "we" person and derives a great deal of value from being part of a team with him as they explore their lives and make their way in the world. The emphasis of the "we-ness" of their relationship turns her on sexually. My friend finds that when he talks in terms of "you" and "I," he just doesn't get the same results—so you can see why he is a real "we" person now!

Couples who don't see themselves as "we" can have sexual difficulties. When one person feels that his or her own interests and needs are dismissed, or that the other person has little investment in the union and an inordinate interest in living as two singles under the same roof, it can impair both desire and arousal. This can even cause impotence in some men. When couples renew their emotional partnership, these problems can start to resolve themselves.

OWNERSHIP: SHARING THE SEXUAL PARTNERSHIP

In healthy marriages, both people wholeheartedly take ownership of whatever they are supposed to do. Both take responsibility for themselves as individuals and as part of the marriage. Jesus said something similar about the way we are to live: "If anyone would come after me, he must deny himself and take up his cross daily and follow me. For whoever wants to save his life will lose it, but whoever loses his life for me will save it" (Luke 9:23–24). In other words, all of us need to take up our own burden in life in order to preserve our lives. Furthermore, as we will see, when both people take ownership in the marriage, it creates a context for healthy sex. Ownership involves shared responsibility, separateness, and self-control. Let's examine what each of these mean.

1. *Ownership means shared responsibility.* Responsibility is an aphrodisiac to a healthy person. For example, when a wife experiences that her husband is who he says he is, is dependable, and shoulders the burdens of his life, she experiences freedom. It frees her from the job of being alone with all the weight of the world and the marriage on her, because she has someone with whom to share the load. It also means that she doesn't have to take responsibility for her partner's life and problems, because he is doing that job for himself. She doesn't have to worry that he

won't keep up his end; nor does she worry that she will have to constantly nag him about duties.

She is also free to be more sexual, as part of good sex is the ability to abandon oneself. Because she's free, she feels lighter and younger and has more emotional energy for sexual connection. When concerns about his responsibility are taken away, sex has room to exist in her mind and imagination. When a wife doesn't feel free—when she has to bear her husband's burdens as well as her own—it can impair her ability to experience desire, arousal, and orgasm. Without freedom from extra responsibility, sex is too costly a luxury.

In addition, when a wife has to shoulder her husband's load, she will begin to feel like she is married to a child—to someone she must take care of and solve problems for, someone who requires her to put out the fires he sets in life. In turn, he will begin to feel he is married to a parent. He will feel controlled and put down. One of the basic requirements God set down for marriage, and sex in marriage, is that it is *for adults only*. Children are not to marry or to have sex. They are developmentally unequipped for either. So when this parent-child dynamic occurs in a marriage, sexual desire and arousal often begin to decrease. This dynamic can also cause a man to struggle with premature ejaculation, a symbol of his sense that he is being treated as an inexperienced, young child.

We have seen and treated many marriages afflicted with this dynamic, and it can be changed, especially when appropriate boundaries are set. Sometimes the change seems magical, as in the case of Sandra and Jim. They came to see me (John) because he did not take sexual initiative with her. She had to do all the pursuing, and even then he was often uninterested. This was a source of great frustration and pain for Sandra. As we talked, we found out that in the rest of their marriage, Jim never disagreed with Sandra on anything. Whether or not he agreed with her opinions on money, the kids, or work, he would comply quietly, even when he had a different viewpoint or was angry with her. We found that Jim was very afraid of losing Sandra's love, and so he would not jeopardize that by standing against her and asserting his individuality, as a spouse should. In other words, Jim was fearful of taking responsibility for his adult feelings and differences with Sandra. He was treating her as if she were a mom whom he could not disappoint. This childlike attitude toward her resulted in a diminishing of his sexual desire for her. Remember, kids don't have sex with their parents.

In addition, there was a second dynamic in their marriage. Not being sexually interested was also a way for Jim to have a little power; if he couldn't say no in life, he could say it in bed. As Sandra understood these issues, she told Jim, "It's okay for you to disagree and get mad at me. I want to be your wife, not your mom." Jim began taking risks with Sandra, and they began to negotiate differences as a couple should—in love, honesty, and respect. As a result, Jim began to feel strong sexual feelings for Sandra, and things began to heat up between them. Later, she reported with a shy smile that their love life had improved dramatically.

Healthy marriages are a mutual covenant of two people, gladly giving up certain liberties and conveniences in order to serve the bond. So when a couple doesn't have a shared sense of responsibility, the relationship is out of balance and often brings dissatisfaction along with sexual problems. Not only can we see this in marriages that have a parent-child dynamic but also in marriages where one person tries to control the other. A controlling mate resists the other mate's freedom, choices, preferences, and opinions, and when the other person says no, a controlling spouse will become angry or withdrawn.

This, too, can cause sexual dysfunction. When there is a large power differential between the two people, and they are not equal in choices and decisions, the controlled spouse does not experience freedom. And as a result, love cannot flourish because love grows out of freedom. This lack of freedom produces fear: fear of loss of love, fear of retribution, fear of the other person's anger. The Bible teaches that love and fear cannot coexist: "There is no fear in love. But perfect love drives out fear, because fear has to do with punishment. The one who fears is not made perfect in love" (1 John 4:18). When you are not made perfect in love, the sexual expression of your love is also bound up in fear. You often withdraw inside of yourself sexually, with diminished desire, little arousal, or an inability to achieve orgasm. Sexuality begins to reemerge only when you and your mate reestablish a more mutual power relationship where neither of you controls the other.

2. *Ownership means separateness.* Ownership, by definition, creates space between two people—separateness. When two people take responsibility for their lives, they are defining themselves as individuals. They are saying, in effect, "I love

you, but I am not you. You have your feelings, values, and opinions, and I have mine. Let's put them together and make something better as they interact." Separateness is simply realizing that while the two in marriage are one flesh, they are still two souls, each of whom must give an account of him- or herself before God one day (2 Corinthians 5:10).

Separateness helps each person in a marriage to assist the other's growth. One has a strength from which the other can learn. One has feedback and perspective that the other one needs to hear. This can certainly cause conflict, but not all conflict is bad (Proverbs 27:17). As the saying goes, "If you never disagree, one of you is not necessary." More than this, however, *separateness creates the longing that is required for sexuality.* Sex is about two people being drawn to each other. Therefore, it follows that for good sex to develop, there needs to be two clear, distinct, well-defined "others"—two distinct people in the equation.

There is space between these two people. Desire and longing have room to grow, and each wants the other person.

When, however, there is little separateness, or when one of the spouses is undefined or highly dependent, it is much more difficult for the other to feel longing. The experience is more that of being smothered by someone's presence or needs. Sexual desire requires someone "over there" whom you can move away from, or closer to. There is freedom, not clinginess. Like the country song says, "How can I miss you when you won't go away?"

This does not mean that separateness is isolation, detachment, and abandonment. While two spouses are separate, they still share their hearts, lives, and loves. In fact, they have to be separate to have hearts, lives, and loves to share. However, while they deeply *love* each other, they *are not each other*. There is a big difference.

3. *Ownership means self-control.* Self-control, a fruit of the Spirit's work in our lives (Galatians 5:23), has to do with things like having our values dictate our behavior and attitudes, as opposed to allowing our impulses, instincts, and appetites to control them. People without self-control tend to be out of control or are controlled by something else. People who are self-controlled make their decisions based on their heart, soul, and mind all coming to a conclusion about something.

Self-control has a great deal to do with sexuality, as sexual impulses are, at their core, oriented to *now.* Like a small child, our raw, unregulated sexual impulses demand instant gratification and release. Sexual impulses left on their own have nothing to do with the feelings, timing, or desires of the other person. However, mature lovers are able to tame their sexual impulses so that they serve the relationship, not just themselves. So if you have self-control, you allow your love and value for your spouse (not your passions) to control your sexual urges, "that each of you should learn to control his own body in a way that is holy and honorable" (1 Thessalonians 4:4). For example, women need time to move from their arousal to orgasm. A husband without self-control can have his orgasm too quickly to allow her to climax. In other situations, a lack of self-control can influence a man to masturbate instead of having intercourse with his wife, as it requires less effort and no consideration of her feelings and situation. In both cases, neither his wife nor the marriage has been served. He has served only himself and his immediate wants.

ACCEPTANCE: EMBRACING REALITY

Acceptance has to do with being able to relate lovingly and without judgment to everything about your mate. It is embracing the reality of his or her strengths and weaknesses, gifts, and imperfections. It does not mean that you approve of everything about your spouse, but it means you are willing to relate to all of him or her without condemnation, even those parts with which you don't agree or of which you don't approve. God in Christ offers us this kind of acceptance (Romans 15:7).

Sexuality requires you to be open and exposed, with all your blemishes and scars. Acceptance creates an environment in which you and your spouse are aware of what the other lacks, but you don't allow those imperfections to stop the flow of love and gratitude for each other. You are so much in love with the character and soul of your beloved that accepting the body is a small thing. However, if you don't convey acceptance, or your partner does not feel acceptable regardless of what you say and do, then he or she will tend to hide, emotionally and sometimes physically. For example, a lack of acceptance can cause a wife not to feel comfortable wearing sexy clothing or to want to make love in total darkness. Lack of acceptance can also diminish desire, arousal, and fulfillment. Acceptance opens us up.

The lack of it shuts down our hearts.

Husbands who don't feel accepted by their wives may have performance anxiety about being sexually competent. Lack of acceptance can drive problems such as impotence and premature ejaculation. However, when husbands and wives work to accept each other without judgment, they can begin to resolve these kinds of problems in their relationship.

Here's an example of what can happen. We know a couple in which the wife, after having two kids, had gotten out of shape. She was not obese, but she did not look or feel the way she wanted to. She felt very unattractive physically, and she was one of those people who tend to be self-critical. Her husband didn't help matters when he nagged her to get back in shape. His pestering joined with her self-condemnation, and she began to feel conditionally loved and under the law of perfection and guilt. As a result, she began to lose her sexual desire.

When they discovered what was going on, her husband rallied to her side. He let her know, "I am really sorry I've made you feel worse about your body. I want you to know that no matter what happens, I love you and I desire only you. Let me know if I put you under the law again, because I don't want you to feel that." His acceptance and grace helped her to feel more loved, and, in time, more sexual. In fact, she began to get back into a good diet and workout program too. Things went well for them after that, but it is important to note that these events happened only after she experienced acceptance from him.

One of the greatest gifts of marriage is that of sex. If you are experiencing difficulties in this wonderful area of life and don't know what to do about them, do not resign yourself to the problem. God has a way, through your growth in him, your marriage, and his resources. Ask him for the next step.

PART III:
BEGIN YOUR JOURNEY TODAY

You are near the end of this book, but you are only at the beginning of the journey God is making for you to recover the joy of your sexual relationship. You may have come to this book not knowing what to do in the face of your problem. We have shown you that God has a way for you, and we have tried to prepare you to walk in that way. In the earlier sections we filled your pack with supplies and put a map in your hands. Now it's time for you to hit the trail. As you do, we leave you with three final words of advice.

WALK IN GRACE. Your first step on the journey, and every subsequent step, is a step into God's grace. Simply put, grace is God's *unmerited favor.* This means that God is on your side. He wants you to resolve your sexual struggle and is committed to work in you, with you, and through you to accomplish it. God loves you completely, and he's going with you every step of the way. He will be your biggest cheerleader.

STEP OUT IN FAITH. You need two strong legs to complete a strenuous hike—right, left, right, left, one after the other. Similarly, in your journey with God, faith is a two-step process. It is both an *attitude* and an *action*. You believe God loves you, but you need to love him in return. You know God will speak to you, but you need to listen attentively. You have faith that God will guide you and protect you, but you need to follow him and submit to his care. Whenever you take a step of *faith* in God, follow it with a step of *action*.

STAY ON THE TRAIL. Now that your feet are moving, let's take one last look at the trail ahead. This is the way God has made for you. It may be strenuous in trying times, but it is also full of discovery and wonder. And the destination is well worth the effort. Here are ten key reminders that will help keep you on the trail and moving forward.

1. Set goals. What do you want God to do for you? Decide now, and be specific. Make your goal as clear and concise as possible so you can envision it, pray about it, and decide on a specific strategy to reach it.

2. Record progress. Write down your goal and put it where you can see it often—on the bathroom mirror, in your daily planner or journal, or elsewhere. Also write down each significant insight as you step toward your goal.

3. Gather resources. Start looking for the people, programs, and organizations that can assist you on the journey. The better your resources, the faster you should reach your goal.

4. Acquire information. Educate yourself on the kind of sexual problem you are facing. Studies show that those who are more knowledgeable about their conditions do better in the treatment of it. They ask insightful questions and sometimes notice things about their condition, feelings, or solutions they might otherwise miss. As much as possible, become an expert in all aspects of your sexual difficulty and its solution.

5. Identify tasks. Give yourself specific assignments: thought patterns to adopt, actions to perform, emotions to express, habits to form, and so forth. Break your tasks into manageable portions and take them one by one.

6. Evaluate progress. Review your progress toward recovery at defined intervals. Are you making headway? If not, why not? Put your evaluation in writing for future reference, and make any necessary adjustments to your plan.

7. Explore preferences. Tailor your plan and tasks to your individual preferences. You will likely have many choices on your journey: counselors, programs, classes, and organizations.

8. Remain flexible. Don't cast your plan in stone. It exists to serve your recovery and growth. If your plan is not getting results over a reasonable period of time, rethink it and make changes. And even when your plan is working, stay alert to ways you can improve it.

9. Pray continually. When you pray, you're not talking to the wall or to yourself. You are talking to God, and he hears you and responds. Prayer is a genuine and powerful ally on your journey. It's not your prayers that have the power; it's God on the other end of the line who has the power to do what you cannot do. Don't take one step without talking to God about it.

10. Pace yourself. This is a journey, not a race. Few changes happen overnight, no matter how hard you work or pray. Give God time to work, and be thankful for the little changes you see.

We are pleased that you are so interested in following God's way to recovery of sexual joy and intimacy. We pray that the God in whom we live, move, and exist will guide and sustain you on the journey, both today and forever. God bless you!

—Henry Cloud, Ph.D.
—John Townsend, Ph.D.
Los Angeles, California

Prayer is

a genuine and

powerful ally

on your journey.

Embark on a
Life-Changing Journey
of Personal and Spiritual Growth

DR. HENRY CLOUD   **DR. JOHN TOWNSEND**

Dr. Henry Cloud and Dr. John Townsend have been bringing hope and healing to millions for over two decades. They have helped people everywhere discover solutions to life's most difficult personal and relational challenges. Their material provides solid, practical answers and offers guidance in the areas of *parenting, singles issues, personal growth,* and *leadership*.

Bring either Dr. Cloud or Dr. Townsend to your church or organization. They are available for:

- Seminars on a wide variety of topics
- Training for small group leaders
- Conferences
- Educational events
- Consulting with your organization

Other opportunities to experience Dr. Cloud and Dr. Townsend:

- Ultimate Leadership workshops—held in Southern California throughout the year
- Small group curriculum
- Seminars via Satellite
- Solutions Audio Club—Solutions is a weekly recorded presentation

For other resources, and for dates of seminars and workshops
by Dr. Cloud and Dr. Townsend, visit:
www.cloudtownsend.com

For other information **Call (800) 676-HOPE (4673)**

Or write to:
Cloud-Townsend Resources
3176 Pullman Street, Suite 105
Costa Mesa, CA